Children of the Earth

"Honoring the People"

Akta Lakota Museum Collection

Produced by St. Joseph's Indian School
Introduction written by Lisa Gerrard
Main copy written by Renee Samson Flood
Edited by Bro. David Nagel, SCJ
Designed and Published by Fenske Companies
Photography by David A. Meyer

Special Thanks to: Dr. Linda Van Hamme, Research Librarian

Library of Congress Catalog Card Number 96-083344
ISBN 1-877976-18-0

For extra Copies of this book contact:
Tipi Press
St. Joseph's Indian School
Chamberlain, South Dakota 57326
1-800-229-5684

Printed in the USA

Akta Lakota Museum
St. Joseph's Indian School
Chamberlain, SD 57326

Introduction

by Lisa Gerrard

It is difficult to conceive, walking the manicured grounds of St. Joseph's Indian School, how many trials the small educational facility has endured in its nearly 70-year history. The blue-green stretch of Missouri River here offers no hint of the dust storms and grasshopper plagues of the Depression years. The tall trees catching the morning sun don't speak of the tornados of 1930 and '31. And the din of children playing in the afternoon makes it hard to hear the crackle of fires destroying or bang of hammers rebuilding through all those years.

For now, all is at peace, but it wasn't always so.

St. Joseph's Indian School opened in September 1927 with 53 Minneconjou children from the Cheyenne River Reservation of north-central South Dakota. Those were troubled years for the proud Teton Sioux tribes who once roamed the Plains. A mere 50 years earlier, they owned all land in the western half of what was to become South Dakota, including the prized Black Hills where Gen. George Custer discovered gold and started the famous 1870's gold rush. The Natives were forbidden by federal law until 1938 to practice their religion or carry on feasts, celebrations and dances. With the buffalo gone, they had come to rely on the Great White Father in Washington for much of their food. No schools had opened on the reservations, so to learn the white man's ways the children began entering schools like St. Joseph's. The rich and complex culture they had built over centuries began to fade.

Eager to help the Indians adapt to this new world, men of faith like Father Henry Hogebach set out to provide education. On mission with the Priests of the Sacred Heart of Germany, Father Henry learned of a former college for sale in Chamberlain. It was perfect but for the price: $40,000 seemed a daunting sum for a small order of frugal priests. But the priests kept their faith, and St. Joseph's opened just in time for the dark 1930s.

The priests received an uncertain welcome. A tornado hit the school in 1930, destroying the barn and damaging other buildings. Then in June 1931, another twister tore through the campus and nearly closed the school forever. Fire erupted in the tornado's wake, leaving only a few sticks of furniture and the old boys' house behind, when the embers finally grew cold.

Luckily most of the children were spending the summer on the reservation, but the nuns had to have a place to house everyone who remained. They wound up cleaning out a chicken coop for themselves and the children. When asked about these strange accommodations, the nuns said, "Our Divine Lord was born in a stable and a chicken coop should be good enough for us."

It seemed the worst was over, but in 1938 two earthquakes shook the school and in 1947, a prairie fire again threatened St. Joseph's existence when it crept dangerously close to Chamberlain.

The Depression brought its own challenges, including dust storms and grasshopper plagues that ruined farmland statewide. To make matters worse, the Franciscan nuns assisting Father Henry were called away to another assignment in 1932. The priests and brothers at St. Joseph's didn't know where to turn. Eventually Father Henry wound up on the steps at the Benedictine Convent in Yankton. As the story goes, he refused to leave until the Mother Superior promised him help. The Mother Superior gave in.

In the 1940s, with the on set of World War II, some of St. Joseph's eighth graders were called away to war. Prices went up and food became scarce. Truckers demanded cash or they would not leave the food they had brought. But then, in the mid-1940s, St. Joseph's luck seemed to change. The drought that gripped the state for seven long years finally broke. Food became more plentiful and by 1949, the school was serving 230 children.

A tremendous building program began in the early 1950s. First came a boys' dormitory and maintenance shop, then a new school building in 1968.

The 1970s brought a new laundry, dining hall and infirmary, while the 1980s saw 16 new Lakota homes for the children. In 1990 the school remodeled its gym so that it now boasts a weight room, game room, and swimming pool.

The school's vision remains the same from its earliest years to give Native American children a better chance at success through education and religious training. But now there's a renewed emphasis on Native American pride, too. St. Joseph's works hard to help students hold onto their valuable culture. The former school building, a round-shaped structure by the river, became the Akta Lakota Museum in 1991. Translated from the Lakota, Akta Lakota means, "honor the people." The only one of its kind in South Dakota, the museum is proud to house hundreds of rare historical artifacts and valuable artwork by Native Americans, some of whom are former St. Joseph's students or aunts, uncles and grandparents of current students.

Each piece in the collection tells a story of the old ways. Each retains a thread linking past with present. St. Joseph's wants to keep these sometimes fragile threads from breaking. And so we celebrate our children's culture here in this book, and celebrate the fact that the school is nearly 70 years old and living in peace, without tornado, fire or grasshopper plague to send us back to the chicken coop.

The school that Father Henry bought in 1927 now serves almost 200 children and employs about 230 teachers, houseparents, counselors, maintenance workers and administrators. A staff physician treats the children's ails, while a staff plumber repairs the sinks. Children from first through eighth grades live together not in dormitories, but in large apartments and homes with child care workers serving as moms and dads away-from-home. High school girls live together on campus and attend the public high school in town, while the older boys make their home off campus in Chamberlain, also attending the public school. A home for college students opened in Mitchell in 1993.

Today the sounds on the river bank are joyful: a football game in the afternoon, children gathered around a table for the evening meal, a trilling voice lifting a sacred song to Wakan Tanka, the Great Spirit, from the sweat lodge on the hill.

The wind whispers in the buffalo grass by the old Missouri, and suddenly we realize how far we have come, together.

AKTA LAKOTA MUSEUM

Native American Cultural Center

Forward

Since 1991, the Akta Lakota Museum has offered visitors a rare and fascinating glimpse at Great Plain's Indian culture, especially that of the Lakota (Sioux). Thousands of interested people have been captivated by the style, scale and richness of the facility and its displays, as they journey through proud heritages of the past into the excitement and adaptation of the modern Lakota way of life.

This quality Native American experience is the only Cultural Center of its kind. St. Joseph's Indian School built the museum collection from gifts received from alumni and friends since the school opened in 1927.

More than just a museum in the traditional sense, the Akta Lakota Museum illuminates the sounds and images of Lakota history by surrounding you with color, music and a rich variety of Native artwork. The Akta Lakota Museum warmly welcomes everyone and looks forward to helping visitors experience a greater appreciation for the Native American way of life in South Dakota, past and present.

Contents

Page 12

1 Children's Collection

The toys and games of Plains Indian children were often a means of learning adult skills. Girls played with miniature tipis made in traditional tribal styles. Dolls were established in small tipis complete with animal skin carpets, cooking gear, cradle boards, and even medicine bundles. In this way, young women were prepared for the responsibilities they would have as adults - constructing, erecting, and taking down tipis, food preparation, making clothing, and caring for children. A young woman also learned the arts of quill embroidery and moccasin making because skill at these crafts brought honor to her family.

For boys, there was also a clear connection between the play of children and the work of adults. Toys such as miniature bows and arrows, and games emphasizing strength, endurance, agility, and horsemanship were used to teach the skills needed by hunters and warriors.

Page 36

2 Artwork

This collection represents a historical portrayal of Plains Indian art from precontract times to the present reflecting both tribal diversity and commonalities in culture, life ways, and art. The development of Plains Indian art reflects adaptive changes in response to historical events as well as the persistence of designs and techniques specific to particular tribes. Art objects are depicted in their cultural context as integral parts of social, religious, and ceremonial systems.

Page 58

3 Everyday Life

Important elements of life were represented in a variety of symbolic ways. Decorative items on clothing were often indicators of prestige, honor, and wealth. A woman wearing a dress covered with elk teeth evidenced the hunting prowess and wealth of her male relatives as well as the high regard in which they held her. Cowrie shells were used on clothing as symbols of fertility.

When a child was born, a cradle board was fashioned by one of the father's sisters as a symbol of her respect for her brother. Cradles were the ultimate in female craftsmanship and brought acclaim to the maker. One of the child's grandmothers also made a small beaded hide bag in the shape of either a turtle or a lizard in which the umbilical cord was placed. The turtle and the lizard were both considered to have protective powers and the amulet bag was intended to protect the child throughout its growing years.

Colors also had symbolic meanings, particularly the four colors representing the four sacred directions. Black represents the West from which come the thunder and the rain. White is for the North and the white cleansing winds of winter. Red is the color of sacredness and wisdom and represents the East from which comes the light of morning. Yellow is the color of the South and represents the maturity and growth of the summer months. (Black Elk)

Children's Collection

Children's Collection

Native American children copied in play the behavior of adult members of their extended families. Girls and boys played out separate roles in society long before they accepted responsibility for adult behavior, but these roles were not as rigid as many historians would have us believe.

The beaded and quilled items in the Children's Collection were made with patient hands, but not necessarily the hands of a mother or female relative. Lakota fathers and uncles made excellent caregivers. When wives were busy cooking, making clothing or tending home fires, children were often with their father or uncle, wrestling about and playing games. He was the prancing horse they climbed up on and he was the rock from which they jumped into the deepest, make believe river. He was the terrifying beast who scared them into giggles

and he was the artist who delighted them with drawings on bark, stone and sand. The patient and devoted Native American father held and still holds a special place in the hearts of his children.

While family members teased him and watched with amusement, uncle fashioned a doll with hide and sinew. On hunting trips he always searched for the most beautiful feathers and shiny stones for his nieces and nephews. A doll might be passed from relative to relative, each adding a finishing touch before it was placed in the arms of a beloved daughter and sometimes a little son. Dolls fashioned in the latest attire wore intricate beaded clothing end Jewelry. The doll carried a faithful copy of a medicine bag or a leather paint bag and knife sheath.

Nowadays, it is rare to find an old doll because the child cuddled, slept on and traveled with her doll until it faded

away. Colors, once bright, meant something special to the dollmaker, but they cannot be interpreted today with authenticity. Red might have meant war to one tribe, while to another tribe, red meant life.

Beaded and quilled balls were stuffed with buffalo hair. After the fur trade began and the missionaries came, yarn balls replaced the beaded ball until finally, the rubber ball with its high bounce became the favorite. Lakota girls erected miniature tipis that grew larger as they got older. Again, the father and uncles were called upon to decorate the tipi with the pretended deeds of the girl's make believe husband. Her little home equaled her mother's domain, with tipi back rests, medicine bundles, and a fire pit, complete with wooden bowls and tiny spoons made from bone. Another important comrade, the family dog, pulled travois packs whenever she moved her pretend camp. Young brothers often amused themselves with imaginary raids on a sister's tipi, until she ran them off. As a girl grew to adolescence, she tolerated these raids less, moving her tipi to hidden locations until finally, worried that her daughter might be caught alone by wayward boys, mother put an end to tipi play.

At an early age the Lakota child learned to respect, love and admire the older members of his family. Grandmothers and Grandfathers, the guardians of language, geneaology and customs, were cherished members of tribal society. Children knew their responsibilities in camp included making sure that elders always had water, firewood and food and to neglect those duties brought shame upon the family.

Willow spears, the favored weapon of young Lakota and Cheyenne boys, filled the skies. They galloped into mock battles, especially reinactments of the "Long Hair Fight," in

which the older boys played Chiefs Crazy Horse or Red Cloud. Of course, nobody wanted to play General Custer. Fathers supplied sons with small quivers, bows and arrows and taught them how to make stone and metal arrow points.

When an old or crippled horse died, father took the ankle bones for his children to play with. Cheyenne and Lakota children spent many happy hours playing games with these particular bones, which represented horses. Other toys included whip and tops that spun around and the popular "Finger bone" game, which required the player to throw connected, hollow, deer bones up in the air and then catch them on a long, thin metal rod or bone pin. "Finger bones" were actually ankle bones from the leg of a deer. Northern Cheyenne boys heated hot iron (pitchfork tines worked best) and then drilled holes in the bones to connect them with strips of rawhide.

Native American children were ingenious at making up games using painted sticks, bones and anything else at hand. At the beginning of the twentieth century, when canned foods were introduced, children used the tin to make a wide variety of toys and decorations. Toys were shared among all the children and it was not customary or allowed for one child to horde a toy for himself. In this way, children learned to respect each other. Whenever there was an argument among the boys, parents stayed out of the fight, allowing the children to work it out for themselves. A child learned to stand on his or her own feet and did not come home expecting sympathy. The result was decreased tension among families in the camp and the young learned to take care of themselves with strength and courage.

Lakota child's beaded navel cord amulet. Turtle for girls. Lizard for boys. CA 1880

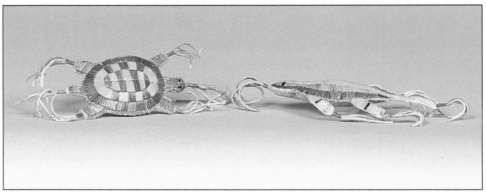

Lakota child's porqupine quill navel cord amulets.C. 1970

Girl's beaded moccaisons. CA 1900-1930

Lakota toy doll and cradle. CA 1880

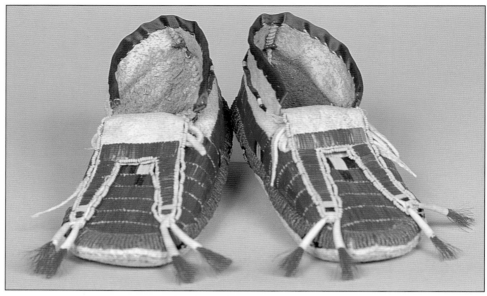

Girl's quilled and beaded moccaisons. CA 1990

Child's beaded moccaisons. CA 1900

Beaded baby baptismal cap. CA 1910

Lakota dolls made by Mary Weasel Bear. CA 1885

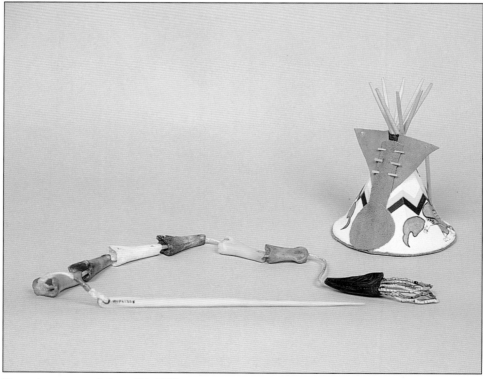

Finger bone game, Lakota. CA 1890

Girl's toy backrest, moccaisons and Tipi bags. CA 1910-1970

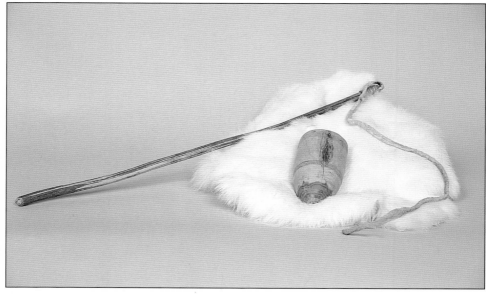

Toy whip and top, Lakota. CA 1910

Lakota dolls, beadwork on buckskin made by Jolene Peterson. CA 1989

Lakota doll quilled and beaded on buckskin. CA 1994

Doll, male beaded on buckskin, Lakota. CA 1880

Boys fully beaded vest, Lakota. CA 1890

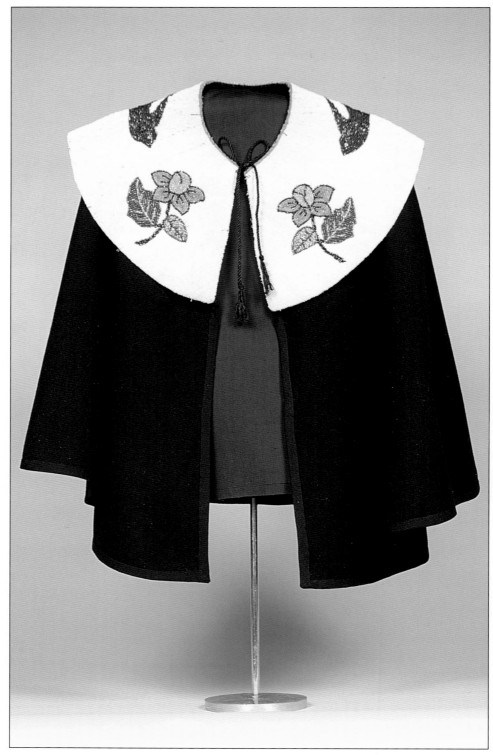

Girl's cape with fully beaded collar. CA 1900

Toy beaded doll cradle, Lakota. CA 1975

Lakota girl's fully beaded yoke dress, Tisa Ravenshead, Cherry Creek, SD. CA 1994

Girl's beaded navel cord amulet, Lakota. CA 1900

Boy's suit, Cheyenne, beaded on buckskin. CA 1900

Girl's cloth dress with beaded bodice, Lakota. CA 1994

Boy's fully quilled and beaded cape, Chris Ravenshead, Cherry Creek, SD. CA 1910

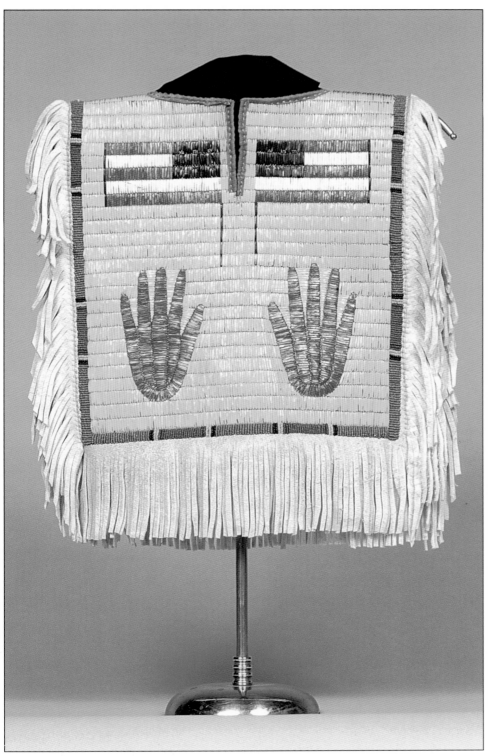

Boy's fully quilled and beaded cape, Chris Ravenshead, Cherry Creek, SD. CA 1910

Purse, fully beaded, Lakota. CA 1890

Child's beaded purse with Elephant, Iroquois. CA 1900

Womans fully beaded purse, Lakota. CA 1910

Akta Lakota Museum Collection

Artwork

Artwork Collection

For thousands of years, Native inhabitants stood on the rim of what has been misnamed Hell's Canyon, in the southern Black Hills of South Dakota. Looking out over this magnificent and mysterious landscape, they watched four rivers flow together, a sacred and symbolic affirmation of the spiritual worldview that supported them. Today, a wild mustang herd roams dry creek beds trimmed with aspen and smooth, multicolored rocks. A deep quiet pervades the canyon floor, with only the cries of nesting swallows to break the ageless silence.

Birds make their homes on steep canyon walls, once the artistic canvas of ancient man, where hundreds of petroglyths tell of an ordered and older world. Human and animal petroglyths show camp sites and they tell of hunting taps, of warfare and of birth and renewal. Carved and painted messages left by ancient Native people have spoken for a longer period of time than any other human communication known to man. In essence, this was Native American artwork in its purest form.

Native men and women still communicate their spirituality, their loves, dreams and visions, and their astonishment at a changed world not of their making. The ancient ones are gone now, but not in spirit. Contemporary Indian artisans carry the same, important messages to those of us who are lucky enough to under-stand their meaning.

In this collection of paintings, beaded and quilled objects, and sculptures in wood, clay, alabaster, bronze and soapstone, can you hear messages in their titles? *Buffalo Is My Spirit, Tipis, Legend of the Iroquots, Eagle-Bear Dreams, They Follow The People, Autumn Hunt, Sioux Spirit, Love Song, Legend of the Three Sisters, Song of the Coyote, Ghost Owl, Sioux Dancer, Keya, Blue Horse, Warrior, The Kill, Chief Spotted Eagle, Buffalo Spirit, Wind in His Hair, Land of the Sioux, and Steamboat Coming.*

Plains Indian art from precontact to the present reflects both tribal diversity and commonalities in culture and religious belief. The Akta Lakota Museum collection shows adaptive changes in response to historical events and a clear persistence of design and technique specific to particular tables.

Historically adaptive changes are seen in beaded horse masks, saddles, bridles, saddle blankets, pistol holsters, pipe bags, knife sheaths and purses, all of which have survived to the present day in Indian Country. An interesting item adapted to its era is the beaded dispatch pouch, circa 1880, possibly designed for an Indian military scout.

Painted hide parfleche bags carried warbonnets and other important belongings to preserve them from moisture damage during river crossings and spring rainstorms. The best clothing, ceremonial articles and paints were protected in this fashion. Parfleche bags worked well in the tipi but when log cabins with damp, earthen floors replaced the fresh air of tipi living, mildew finally took its toll. By the late 1940s, most of the older parfleche bags had wasted away and were replaced by suitcases.

Although the Plains tribes adapted and readapted over the centuries, there is a striking statement of strength and identity among all indigenous peoples of the Americas and this is especially true of Plains Indian art, which captures the Indian male as warrior, as provider and as the ultimate protector. He is often honored in paintings reflecting his image in clouds, signifying a continued spirit vigilance.

Another basic unity shared by all plains tribe es was a common means of sustenance, the buffalo. This important animal thrives today in Native artwork. In the precontact era, buffalo were needed for a healthy life. At birth, the child was swaddled in young calfskin and buffalo hides were used for robes, clothing, tipis, boats, and drums. Weapons were made by fastening wet strips of hide to stone war clubs and arrows to their shafts.

Woven buffalo hair made strong rope or was used to stuff cradleboards, saddles, pillows and balls. Buffalo horn became spoons, ribs became sleds and small bones became awls. Dried buffalo meat, deer and elk, wild turnips and berries provided a healthy diet and buffalo manure was an important source of fuel when trees were scarce.

The thick chest or brisket hide of the buffalo made useful bowls when cut in a circle and then molded and dried over a post. A hole punched near the rim before drying made it easier to hang up when not in use. Men and women alike hung small wooden bowls from their belts. They used the vessels to drink water, eat soup, carry beads etc. It was not as durable as the larger buffalo brisket bowl because with every step, it swung from side to side, making the hole bigger, until it finally snapped off the rim.

It is said the last wild buffalo was killed around 1885, but today, most tribes on the Great Plains have a growing buffalo industry. Every year the buffalo still provides his people with meat and hides and in the silence of winter evenings, his stories are told and retold for future generations.

"Steamboat Coming" Acrylic, Del Iron Cloud, Hunkpapa Sioux. Former St. Joseph student.

"Tipi's" Mixed media, Don Ruleaux, Oglala Sioux.

"Blue Horse" Watercolor on paper, Don Montileaux, Oglala Sioux.

"They Follow the People" Bornze,
King Kuka, Blackfeet.

"Warrior" Alabaster, Al Belgarde,
Turtle Mountain.

"Eagle-Bear Dreams" Pottery, Nick Halsey, Lakota. Former St. Joeseph student.

Artwork

"Grandmother" Watercolor, Robert Penn, Sicangu Lacotah / Omaha.

"Unpo" (Daybreak) Airbrush, Michael Willcuts, Minniconjou Sioux.

"Circle of Hope" Acrylic on canvas, John Beheler, Yanktonai Sioux. Former St. Joseph student.

Artwork

"Grandfather" Watercolor, Robert Penn, Sicangu Lacotah / Omaha.

"Chief Spotted Eagle" Wood,
Alfred Decotau, Turtle Mountain.

"Keya" Bronze, Larry De Coteau, Turtle Mountain.
Former St. Joseph student.

"Love Song" Bronze, Larry De Coteau, Turtle Mountain. Former St. Joseph student.

"Echoes of Our Grandparents" Acrylic on canvas, Alfreda Beartrack, Lower Brule Sioux.

"Chief Dirty Kettle" Acrylic on canvas, Mark Powers, Brule / Yanktonai Sioux.

"Song of the Coyote" Bronze, Alfred Ziegler, Lakota. Former St. Joseph student.

"Red Bear" Watercolor and Acrylic on canvas, Andrea Two Bulls, Oglala Lakota.

"Tatanka Ska Oyate" Acrylic on canvas, Robert Freeman, Brule / Yankton Sioux.

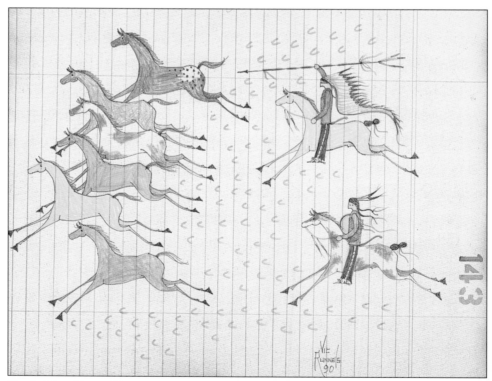

"Steals Many Horses" Dye on raw canvas, Vic Runnels, Oglala Sioux.

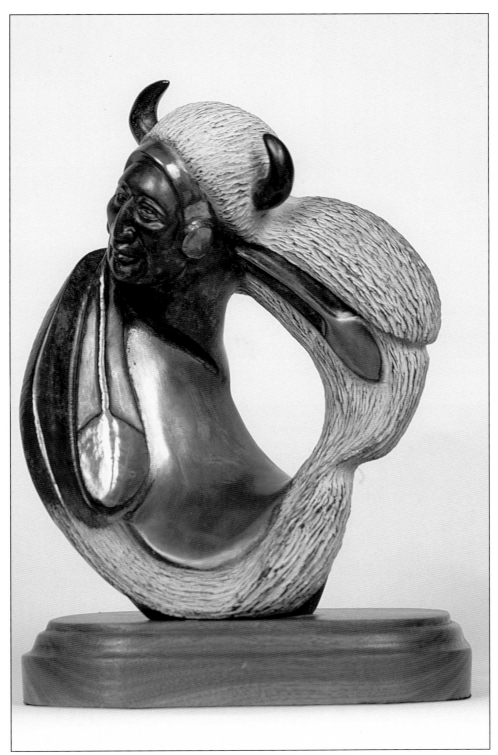

"Buffalo Spirit" Bronze, Alfred De Coteau, Turtle Mountain.

"Land of the Sioux" Acrylic, Daniel Long Soldier, Oglala Sioux.

"Little Sioux" Acrylic, pencil and tempera, Jim Yellowhawk, Lakota/Iroquois.

"The Council" Watercolor on canvas, Robert Freeman, Luiseno/Santee Sioux.

Everyday Life

Everyday Life Collection

At least six indigenous language groups lived on the Great Plains, a wide range of territory extending from northern Alberta and Saskatchewan, Canada, south into Texas. Tribes included the Lakota/ Dakota/ Nakota, Cheyenne, Arapaho, Crow, Blackfeet, Plains Cree, Comanche, Pawnee and many, many others, all with different customs and religious beliefs.

By the 17th century, Native Americans adapted horses from the southwest and the fur trade had increased barter in beads, shells, and items such as cooking pots, traps, blankets, needles, thread, guns and cloth. The buffalo was not necessarily easier to hunt with a heavy gun than with bows and arrows, but the horse made it possible to cover larger distances in search of food.

Although the Lakota and Northern Cheyenne followed buffalo herds, the Black Hills in South Dakota remained sacred to them, especially Bear Butte, Wind Cave and Devil's Tower in Wyoming. No matter how far they ranged within the Great Plains region, they resumed to Bear Butte at various times during the year for religious renewal ceremonies and vision quests For many traditional Native people, Bear Butte was and still is their Holy Land.

Religious symbols and designs in Native American clothing and art changed dramatically from one tribe to another but a unifying commonality within every tribe was their love for children. Of particular interest in the Akta Lakota Museum collection are beaded and quilled cradleboards. For hundreds, perhaps thousands of years, Indian children were strapped to cradleboards to view the world from an upright, adult position. The long, wooden points at the top provided a safety measure during journeys when the cradleboard hung from a saddlehorn. If a horse bucked the little passenger into the air, the pointed ends would either stick into the snow, or at least stop the board from rolling. Mothers hung cradleboards on branches so babies could watch and enjoy their siblings at play. They were kept dry by diapering with cloth or rawhide filled with shredded willow bark moss or soft cattail down.

A tightly wrapped infant could not grab, chew or swallow harmful objects. His back and neck grew strong and straight at a young age and the tight swaddling kept him surprisingly snug, safe and calm. In the 1890s, government matrons assigned to reservations complained to government officials that cradleboards produced deformities. Almost overnight the use of cradleboards died out. Since the 1970s however, the cradleboard has seen a resurgence and it is often used today at social gatherings and as wall decorations in Native

American homes.

A beautiful item in the Children of the Earth Collection is a beaded bag made to store the umbilical cord of a child, circa 1890. A girl's pouch was beaded in the form of a turtle, while a boy's pouch was formed in the shape of a lizard. As with other cultural artifacts, shapes and colors varied from tribe to tribe.

The 1890 girl's turtle pouch in this collection depicts two American flags with a Cross above it. Below the flags is a heart. It was not unusual for Native people to blend traditional religion with Christianity, as they often do today. The care of a child's umbilical cord was of crucial importance to Native parents. The Lakota mother took special care to suspend the beaded bag on her child's cradleboard after offering prayers for longevity and the continued good health of her baby. When a child was old enough to walk, she hung the bag on his belt. This ancient custom representing familial love and tribal devotion is still practiced today in rural Indian Health Hospitals as well as in large metropolitan medical centers across the country.

The life path of a Lakota child was a continuous daily process of spiritual development. It began from the moment of birth and for the rest of his life he yearned for knowledge and wisdom. There were no written rules or laws, no jails, no schools and no courts. The family was the source of education including grandparents, uncles, aunts, cousins and many adopted relatives. The "tiyospaye" or extended family, could mean as many as 300 people. From relatives, the young learned proper conduct, and the skills they would need to ensure the safety and continued well being of the tribe.

At morning light, grandfather's prayer song stirred the family. An eagle's flight was uncle's inspiration to pray and father offered tobacco and prayer for the spirits of animals he needed to feed his family. Finally, at bedtime, mother's gentle prayer ended the day. The spiritual life of man, woman and child on the Great Plains was interrelated with the clan, the tribe, the environment and every living thing on earth.

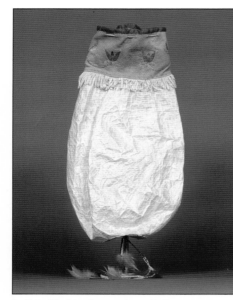

Buffalo Bladder Bag with quill decoration. CA 1973

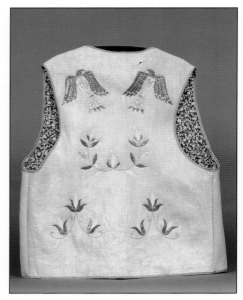

Quilled mans vest, Santee Sioux. CA 1975

Eagle Feather War Bonnet, Lakota. CA 1890

Mans beaded scout coat. CA 1970

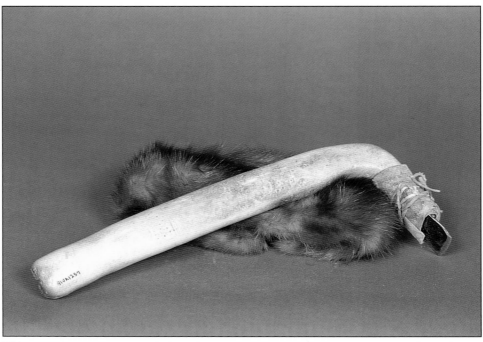

Elkhorn hide flesher with metal blade. CA 1850

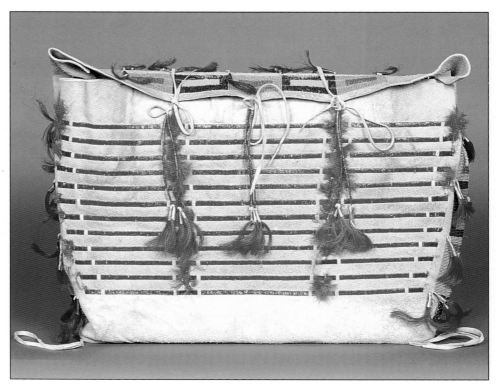

Tipi bag, used for storage, beaded and quilled, Mary Weasel Bear. CA 1885

Lakota womans cow hide work bag and deer bone hide flesher. CA 1890

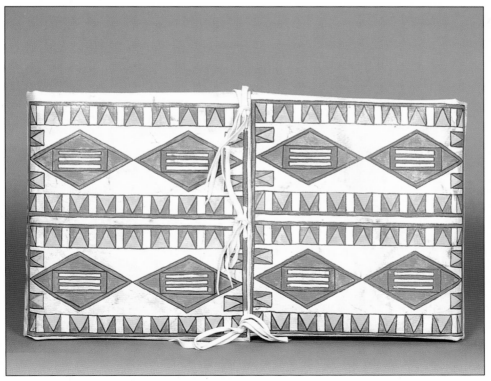

Painted rawhide suitcase, Lloyd One Star. CA 1995

Womans saddle crow. CA 1870

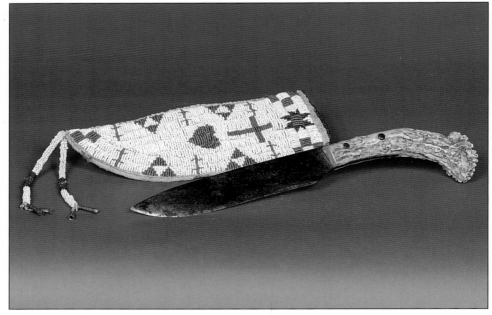

Lakota beaded knife case with knife. CA 1900

Painted rawhide medicine cylinder. CA 1870

Painted rawhide trunk. CA 1880

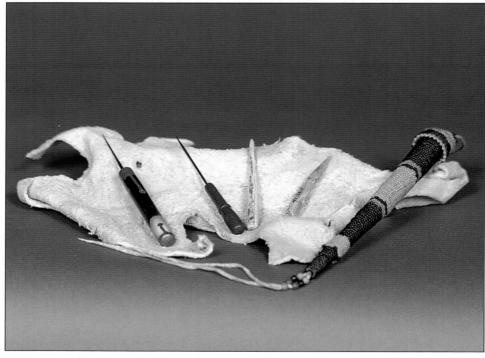

Various type of awls used for sewing. CA 1890

Cheyenne mans fully beaded vest, Mrs. Smokey Door.

Woman's bone breast plate. CA 1880

Fully beaded saddle bags. Tisa Ravenshead, Cherry Creek, SD. CA 1995

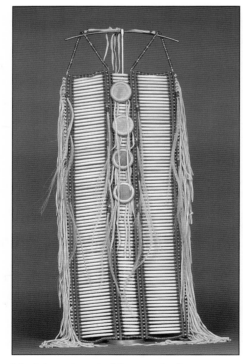

Man's bone breast plate worn in dances. CA 1994

Beaded dispatch pouch. CA 1880

Beaded horse bridle, Lakota, Tisa Ravenshead, Cherry Creek, SD. CA 1994

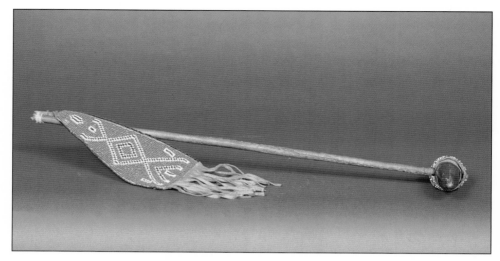

Beaded dance club, Lakota. CA 1890

Child's cherry pounder and base. CA 1880

Saddle blanket, beaded on buckskin. Bluebird collection. CA 1885

Stone effigy dance club, mountain sheep carving. CA 1890

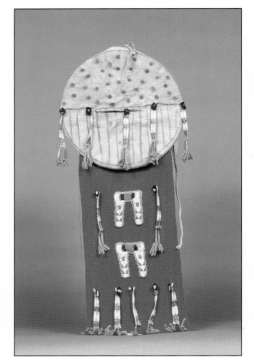

Child's dance shield, Lakota. CA 1990

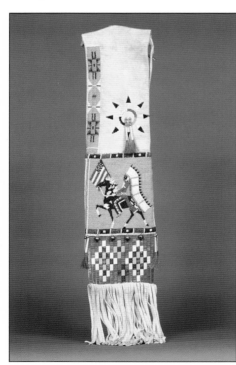

Beeded and quilled tobacco bag, Jimmy Little Wounded, Eagle Butte, SD. CA 1980

Tobacco bag, beaded and quilled, Lakota. CA 1994

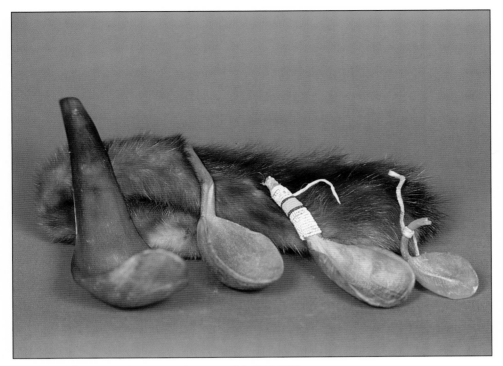

Baffalo, cow and sheep horn carved spoons. CA 1960-1880

Rawhide bowl with stone headed rawhide wrapped handle and stone base used in making Wasnl. CA 1850

Hawk-tail dance fan. CA 1960

Wood burl bowl with cow horn spoon. CA 1830-1880

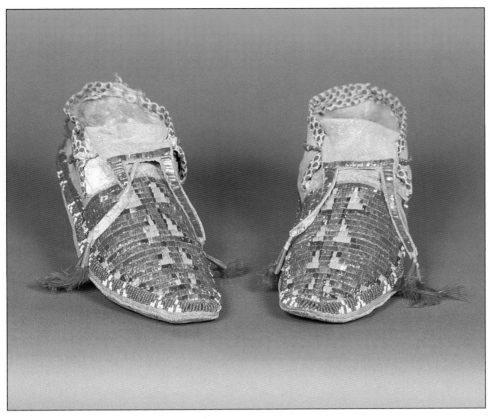

Man's quilled and beaded moccaisons. CA 1900

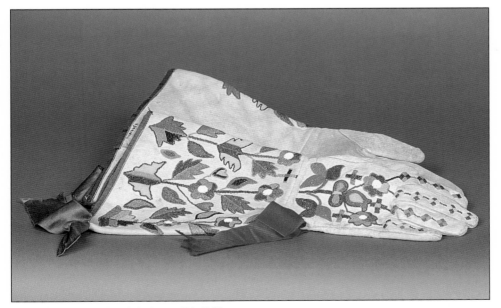

Santee Sioux mens beaded gloves. CA 1865

78

Catunite pipe with quilled wood stem. CA 1890

Quilled and beaded horse mask, Chris Ravenshead, Cherry Creek, SD. CA 1995

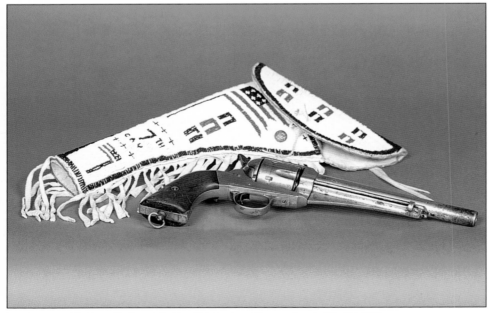

Beaded pistol holster, Esther Afraid of Lightning, Cherry Creek, SD. CA 1979

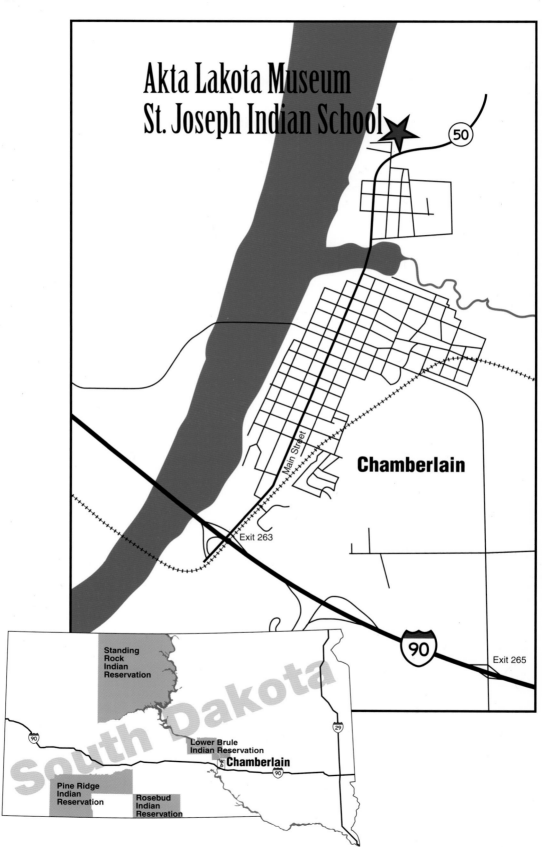

Akta Lakota Museum
St. Joseph Indian School

Chamberlain

50

Main Street

Exit 263

90

Exit 265

South Dakota

Standing Rock Indian Reservation

Lower Brule Indian Reservation

Chamberlain

Pine Ridge Indian Reservation

Rosebud Indian Reservation

29

90